A Parisian Fairytale: Christiaan Dior's Journey from Art to Fashion to Empire (Art Fiction Books)

A novel-like biography of Christian Dior, his artistic inspirations, and the sister who shaped his greatest creation

C. Fontaine Marchand

Contents

Prologue: The Whisper of Granville's Gardens	1
1. The Artistic Dreamer in Paris	5
2. From Sketches to Haute Couture	12
3. Shadows of War and Family Ties	21
4. The Birth of the New Look	27
5. Fragrance of Memories	32
6. Blossoming into an Empire	37
7. The Ghost at the Door	41
8. The Architect and the Man Behind Dior	50
9. Legacy of Elegance	57
Epilogue: The Eternal Fragrance	61
Appendices:	65
Timeline of Significant Events in Christian and Catherine Dior's Lives	67
Fashion Terms	69

Prologue: The Whisper of Granville's Gardens

The Scent of Destiny

The wind carries the scent of roses. It drifts through the gardens of *Villa Les Rhumbs*, curling between ivy-covered trellises, rustling the golden daffodils, and settling in the tangled curls of a boy wandering through the blooms. **Christian Dior inhales deeply**, letting the fragrance flood his senses—velvety, warm, a whisper of something both comforting and intoxicating.

He is not yet a designer, nor even a dreamer of dresses. He is merely a boy with **a sharp eye for beauty and a heart tuned to the delicate music of the world around him**.

His fingers brush against the petals of a **soft pink rose**, feeling the silk-like texture beneath his touch. It is as if the flower is telling him a secret, something only he can understand. He does not know it yet, but this moment will stay with him. **This scent, this feeling—it will become a part of him.**

His Mother's Garden: A Place of Order and Elegance

A little further down the path, **Madeleine Dior moves with quiet grace**, the hem of her pale linen dress skimming the dewy grass. Her straw hat shields her from the morning sun, but soft wisps of dark hair escape in the breeze. She hums as she tends to her beloved roses, hands dusted with earth yet delicate as they work.

Christian watches her from behind a row of trimmed hedges, mesmerized. **His mother is elegance itself, effortless in the way she moves, in the way she tends to beauty.**

She plucks a spent bloom from the bush and sighs. **"A flower must be cared for, Christian. It must be shaped, nurtured. Only then does it reach perfection."**

He nods solemnly, though he does not yet fully understand. He only knows that the roses are **perfect because of her**, that their existence depends on the gentle hands that shape them. **One day, he will create beauty in the same way—by shaping, refining, designing.**

A Painter's Eye, A Designer's Soul

Christian's mind is a palette of colors. **He sees the garden as an artist sees a canvas**—splashes of crimson poppies against a backdrop of emerald leaves, the deep purple of an iris trembling in the wind, the soft blue sky above stretching like an endless silk ribbon.

He does not yet sketch, but **his imagination is painting**. He wonders if there is a way to **wear** these colors, to carry them not just in his memory but against the skin, like a second nature.

Later, as a man, he will find his answer: silk gowns dyed in the shades of his mother's roses, perfume bottles capturing the scent of this very morning.

The Wind and the Whisper: A Promise of the Future

A strong gust **rushes through the garden**, sending petals dancing into the air. Christian closes his eyes. He lets the wind push against him, feeling it as something more than just air—**it is a whisper, a prophecy.**

He has always believed in signs, though he does not yet have the words for it. This moment, the scent of roses, the way the wind curls around his small frame—it is an omen, an unseen force guiding him toward a future that has not yet revealed itself.

His mother kneels before him, pressing **a fresh rose into his small hands**. He holds it carefully, as though it is the most precious thing in the world.

"Do you know what this rose is called?" she asks.

He shakes his head.

"**It is a Rosa centifolia. The hundred-petaled rose.**" She smiles. "It is rare, delicate. But it is strong, too. Like all beautiful things, it must fight to bloom."**

He nods, storing the words away in his heart. One day, he will remember them when he steps onto the grand stage of fashion. When he creates his first perfume. When he sends his first collection down the runway.

For now, though, he is simply a boy in his mother's garden, a boy who loves flowers and colors, a boy who does not yet know that the scent of roses will follow him **for the rest of his life.**

Shadows on the Horizon

The garden is a place of magic, but it will not last forever.

Soon, the Diors will lose *Villa Les Rhumbs*, victims of **financial ruin**. The family will fracture, and Christian will be forced to find a new path, one paved with uncertainty and risk.

But he does not know that yet.

For now, he stands **wrapped in the scent of roses**, bathed in the golden morning light, listening to the whispers of the garden. One day, he will bottle this moment. One day, the world will know this scent as **Miss Dior**.

And with that, his fairytale will begin.

The Artistic Dreamer in Paris

Arrival in Paris: A New World Unfolds (1917)
The streets of Paris **hummed with life**, a symphony of movement and voices, horse-drawn carriages and early automobiles vying for space, their wheels rattling over cobblestones still wet from the morning's rain. The air smelled of **freshly baked bread, damp stone, and something else—something intangible but unmistakable: ambition.**

From inside the Dior family's **elegant black carriage**, ten-year-old **Christian Dior** pressed his forehead against the cold window, watching the city unfold before him. This was not **Granville**, where the sea whispered against the cliffs, where roses and jasmine grew wild in his mother's garden. **This was Paris.**

The carriage halted in front of their new home—a **magnificent Haussmannian building in the 16th arrondissement, its limestone façade bathed in the golden light of late afternoon.**

Christian hesitated on the doorstep. He could hear his father's voice—**Maurice Dior, ever pragmatic, already speaking to the driver about business.** His mother, **Madeleine, graceful and poised**, adjusted the pearl buttons on her gloves before stepping inside.

"Come, Christian," she said gently, looking over her shoulder.

Still, he hesitated. He had always felt safe in Granville, tucked away in his mother's gardens. But **Paris was a different world**, its pace quicker, its energy sharper. And yet, something stirred in him—a **thrill, an unspoken certainty that here, something awaited him.**

This was the city where **things happened.**

If Paris belonged to his father's ambitions, **Christian belonged to its art.**

Maurice Dior had **no patience for frivolity.** He had mapped out a future for his son—**diplomacy, business, respectability.**

But Christian had no interest in politics or banking. **Numbers did not move him.**

Colors did. Lines. The way shadows danced in the corners of grand buildings. **Beauty, in all its forms.**

One day, his mother took him to **the Louvre,** a visit that was meant to be a pleasant afternoon but instead became **a revelation.**

Inside, the museum was cool and vast, its towering ceilings and endless corridors making him feel both **small and infinite at the same time.**

He wandered from room to room, his footsteps slow, as if he were walking through a dream. **And then, he saw her.**

"La Grande Odalisque."

The painting stopped him in his tracks. **Jean-Auguste-Dominique Ingres' masterpiece—sensual, surreal, draped in folds of fabric that seemed to spill off the canvas.**

He was mesmerized. Not just by the woman, but by the **way she was framed, the way the fabric moved around her body, how every stroke of the brush sculpted something more than just an image.**

His mother's voice was soft beside him. **"Beautiful, isn't she?"**

Christian could not answer. He simply stared, feeling something inside him shift, as if he had just discovered a secret written in the language of color and form.

From that moment, he knew.

That night, he sketched by candlelight—**not people, not landscapes, but dresses.**

He did not yet understand why. **Only that it felt right.**

By his late teens, **Christian had perfected the art of deception.**

He feigned interest in his father's business discussions, nodding when expected, playing the role of an obedient son. But at night, **he slipped away into another world.**

The world of **Montparnasse.**

Here, in the dim glow of streetlamps, artists huddled in **smoke-filled cafés**, debating surrealism over glasses of wine, their fingers smudged with ink and charcoal.

At **Le Dôme, La Rotonde, Café de Flore**, Christian listened.

He listened to **Jean Cocteau**, whose words moved like poetry. **He met Picasso**, who spoke of revolution in brushstrokes.

"Forget perfection," Picasso told him once. *"Perfection is a trap."*

Christian disagreed. He loved **balance, elegance, harmony.** But the idea lingered—**that art was not only about representation but about emotion, reinvention.**

At home, his father grew suspicious of his late nights.

"A Dior does not live like a starving artist," Maurice warned.

Christian said nothing. **He was already too far gone.**

By 1928, **Christian Dior had made a decision.**

If he could not be an artist, he would champion them.

Paris was **teeming with visionaries**, painters who saw the world through fractured glass, sculptors who carved emotion into stone, poets who spoke in riddles and wine-stained whispers. Christian, ever the observer, had spent years at their side—watching, listening, absorbing. But **he wanted to do more than just witness genius. He wanted to give it a home.**

His father, **Maurice Dior**, was not an easy man to convince.

"An art gallery?" Maurice sighed, looking over his spectacles, his

tone caught between exasperation and resignation. *"If you must waste your time, Christian, at least do it properly."*

It was the closest thing to approval Christian would ever receive. And it was enough.

Thus, in a quiet corner of **Rue La Boétie, the Galerie Jacques Bonjean was born.**

The space was **modest but elegant**, its walls soon adorned with canvases that defied convention. **The surrealist landscapes of Dalí twisted reality into dreamlike distortions, Giorgio de Chirico's eerie cityscapes loomed with unseen stories, and the sharp geometry of Georges Braque's cubist compositions disrupted expectations.**

Christian curated not just with an eye for talent, but with **an understanding of movement, of form, of the unspoken dialogue between art and its observer.**

The gallery soon became more than just a place to view paintings.

At night, it transformed.

It became **a salon of ideas, a sanctuary where writers, poets, and musicians gathered**, their conversations curling through the air like smoke. **Absinthe and ambition fueled their debates**, and the room thrummed with the electricity of possibility.

Christian was always there, listening in the shadows, his sharp eyes darting between canvases and conversations. He was studying, not just the artists but their work—**the way color directed emotion, how shadows softened angles, how negative space created meaning.**

Then, one evening, something startled him.

He had been watching a woman, a **muse draped in silk**, as she leaned against the wall, absently touching the sleeve of her dress. The fabric caught the dim light, **folding, bending, cascading in a way that mimicked the very compositions he had studied in the paintings behind her.**

His breath caught.

Fashion was not so different from art.

The way a painting guided the eye, the way a sculpture curved, the way light and shadow played on a canvas—**it could all be translated into fabric. Into silhouette. Into movement.**

The thought struck him **like a premonition.**
He didn't yet understand the depth of this revelation. He only knew that **something inside him had shifted forever.**

Then, the world **cracked open.**

The **1929 stock market crash** sent shockwaves across the world. Paris, once a city brimming with creativity and indulgence, began to suffocate under the weight of economic collapse.

Christian saw it happening in slow motion.

The collectors who had once filled his gallery **vanished overnight. The paintings, which had once seemed untouchable, became mere objects again—objects that could no longer be afforded.**

One by one, **the masterpieces were removed.**

The gallery, once buzzing with life, fell silent. The **hollow sound of frames being unhooked from walls, the dull scrape of nails being pried loose—it was a funeral, and Christian was the only mourner.**

He ran his fingers over the empty spaces where art had once existed. **Ghosts lingered there, whispers of lost ambition.**

And then, the final blow came.

His father's business collapsed. The once-proud Maurice Dior, **who had built an empire in fertilizer and chemicals, watched his fortune crumble to dust.**

Everything—the gallery, the security, the carefully laid plans—was gone.

On a **gray, rain-soaked evening,** Christian **locked the gallery doors for the last time.**

He turned the key slowly, feeling **as if he were closing a part of himself inside.**

Afterward, he wandered through Montmartre.

But even the cafés felt different now.

The conversations had grown quieter. **The artists no longer spoke** of revolution, of breaking boundaries, of new movements and bold strokes. They spoke of rent. Of hunger. Of survival.

The laughter was gone. The city had lost its color.

For the first time, **Christian Dior had nothing.**

No fortune. No career. **No future.**

He drifted.

For months, **Christian moved from one small job to another, sketching to survive.**

At first, it was just a means to an end—quick illustrations sold for a few francs, sketches for department store advertisements, whatever scraps of work he could find.

But something happened.

In the quiet hours of the evening, as he traced lines onto paper, **he began to notice something new.**

A dress was not just fabric.

A gown's silhouette could be **sculpted like a statue.**

The drape of silk could **carry the weight of a story.**

The movement of a garment could be **captured like brushstrokes on a canvas.**

Fashion, he realized, **was art.**

The idea bloomed inside him like **a long-dormant seed finally breaking through the soil.**

One evening, Christian sat by the Seine, **his sketchbook open on his lap.**

The city **stretched before him, golden lights flickering against the river's dark surface.** Paris was still beautiful, still alive, despite everything it had lost.

He reached for his pencil, hesitated.

For years, he had drawn **paintings, sculptures, buildings—things meant to be admired from a distance.** But tonight, his hand moved differently.

He did not draw a painting.

He did not sketch a sculpture.

He drew **a dress.**

A long, sweeping silhouette, fabric cascading like water, a design built for movement, for beauty, for life.

His heart pounded.

"This is it."

He did not yet know that one day, the world would know his name.

That he would redefine fashion, create **a revolution in femininity, elegance, and silhouette.**

That he would give women something more than clothing—**he would give them dreams.**

All he knew, in that moment, **was that he had found his true calling.**

And for now, **that was enough.**

From Sketches to Haute Couture

Paris had lost its luster.

The grand avenues were still there, the balconies still adorned with wrought-iron railings, the streetlights still glowing at dusk, but **the city had become quieter, more subdued**. Wealth had disappeared from the salons, replaced by a cautious frugality. The war had not yet come, but **poverty had already begun its slow march through the streets**.

Christian Dior felt it in his bones.

He **had no gallery, no money, no inheritance to fall back on**. His father's once-prosperous business had crumbled, and with it, the life that had once been laid out so clearly for him. He was adrift, moving from one odd job to another, clinging to the only skill he had left—**his ability to draw**.

And so, he sketched.

In a **tiny rented room near Montmartre, lit by a single flickering candle**, he hunched over his desk, tracing silhouette after silhouette with the precision of a painter, but with the hunger of a man who needed to eat.

At first, it was survival.

He **sold his fashion sketches to small designers, to seamstresses, to magazines that barely paid enough for a cup of coffee. The money came in trickles—sometimes enough for a meal, sometimes just enough to buy more paper.

But something strange happened.

His sketches were **selling faster.** His name was whispered in the back rooms of dress shops, in the halls of couturiers who barely knew him but were beginning to take notice.

And then, **one afternoon, in a small tailor's shop, he overheard the name that would change his life.**

"Did you hear?" one of the assistants murmured. *"Piguet is looking for someone."*

Christian felt his breath catch.

Robert Piguet.

The name was legendary. His designs were **pure elegance— nothing wasted, nothing excessive.** If anyone understood the art of refinement, it was Piguet.

That night, **Christian pressed his best sketches into a leather folder, straightened his secondhand suit, and walked toward destiny.**

The first time **Christian Dior stepped into the house of Robert Piguet**, he felt something shift inside him.

This was **not** the chaotic, ink-stained world of the Montparnasse cafés, where artists argued about form and abstraction over cigarette smoke and unfinished paintings. **This was something entirely different.**

The atelier was **a place of quiet discipline, of perfectly timed stitches and measured silence, where the language spoken was not in words, but in fabric.** Every seam, every dart, every delicate fold had **purpose.** There was no room for excess, no space for anything but precision.

Robert Piguet himself stood in the center of it all.

He was **a man of sharp wit and sharper instincts, his mere presence commanding respect.** He did not fuss over details—he dissected them with a glance, deciding in an instant whether a design was worthy or a failure. His suits were always impeccably tailored, his movements deliberate, his voice low but unwavering.

On Christian's **first day,** Piguet greeted him with a single sentence:

"Elegance," he said, **without looking up from the fabric in his hands,** *"is knowing when to stop."*

Christian held his breath.

He had spent years admiring **the excess of avant-garde painters, the wild brushstrokes of the Surrealists, the deliberate chaos of Cubism.** But this—this was something else.

This was **restraint.**

This was **mastery.**

And Christian, for the first time, **understood what it meant.**

The first few weeks were **humbling.**

Christian was no novice—he had spent years sketching dresses, selling his illustrations to survive. But here, in the **hushed, disciplined world of Piguet's atelier,** he realized how little he truly knew.

His first sketches were met with a sigh.

"Too much," Piguet would say, barely glancing at the paper before setting it aside.

Christian would go back, **erase a flourish, remove an embellishment, simplify a silhouette.**

He would present it again.

"Still too much."

It **infuriated him at first.** He had always believed in **romanticism, in grandeur, in the sweeping gestures of art.**

But Piguet was teaching him something else entirely.

"Elegance is not what you add, Dior. It's what you take away."

And so, he learned.

He learned to **strip away the unnecessary,** to let fabric fall naturally instead of forcing it into artificial structures. He learned **that a single pleat could change an entire silhouette, that restraint was not a limitation, but a skill.**

His lines became **sharper. His vision clearer.** His designs began to reflect **not only beauty, but balance.**

And then, one day, **Piguet did not set his sketch aside.**

He studied it for a long moment, tracing a single finger over the design before nodding.

"Now, this," he said, a rare flicker of approval in his voice, *"is elegance."*

Christian felt **a thrill run through him.**

For the first time, he had done more than just draw a beautiful dress. **He had designed something timeless.**

Soon, his sketches **were no longer just drawings in the margins of fashion magazines.**

They were in the ateliers, **on cutting tables, in the hands of seamstresses who brought them to life with delicate, practiced precision.**

Christian spent hours hovering over them as they worked, watching **how fabric moved, how stitches disappeared into seams, how silk flowed like water.**

The first time he saw one of **his designs take shape**—a sleek black crepe dress with a soft neckline, fitted just enough to enhance the body without restricting it—**he felt something almost indescribable.**

It was the **same feeling he had as a child in Granville**, watching his mother tend to her roses, shaping them, guiding them, never forcing them to be anything other than what they were meant to be.

This was **creation.**

And Paris began to take notice.

His name began appearing in **the glossy pages of Vogue**, his designs appearing alongside those of Paris's most revered couturiers.

Women stopped in front of boutique windows, **their gloved hands pressed to the glass, admiring the dresses Christian had designed.** They whispered his name in hushed admiration, passing it like a secret between them.

"Dior," they murmured, intrigued by this new designer who understood something **that had been forgotten in the noise of modern fashion—grace.**

For the first time, Christian **felt something exhilarating—recognition.**

He was **on the cusp of something great.**

He could feel it in his bones.

But **fate had other plans.**

The city, despite its glamour, was **holding its breath.**

Christian saw it in the way people hurried through the streets, in the way conversations drifted toward the same ominous topic:

War.

The newspapers reported **gathering tensions in Europe**, warnings of invasions, of a storm that was brewing just beyond the horizon.

But inside Piguet's atelier, the world remained untouched.

Fabrics were draped, gowns were sewn, fashion continued as if beauty could defy the dark cloud hanging over Paris.

Then came the day Christian dreaded.

A letter, pressed into his hands.

His name, neatly typed, beneath the official emblem of the French government.

He had been conscripted into military service.

He ran his fingers over the paper, his chest tightening.

The atelier, the sketches, the fabric, the world of beauty he had just begun to understand—**he had to leave it all behind.**

Piguet placed a hand on his shoulder.

"Come back to us when the war is over," he said simply. *"Paris will still need beauty."*

Christian swallowed hard.

He didn't know when—**or if—he would return.**

All he knew was that the world outside **was about to change.**

And with it, **his destiny.**

The sky was impossibly blue on the day war was declared.

It should have been gray, heavy with rain, the way it always was in moments of dread. But no—**the sun shone, its warmth untouched** by the tension that gripped Paris, as if the heavens themselves were oblivious to the catastrophe unfolding below.

Christian Dior stood at his window, watching the city move **as if in slow motion.** Women hurried down the streets clutching newspapers with bold, black headlines, their gloves trembling as they turned the pages. Café tables, once filled with loud debates on poetry and fashion, sat half-empty, the voices that remained hushed. **Something unseen had shifted in the very bones of the city.**

Paris held its breath.

At first, **nothing changed.**

The Germans were still far away. The shops remained open. The Seine continued its quiet, endless flow. **Life carried on—but with an unspoken hesitation, a pause between each breath.**

Then, **the draft notices arrived.**

One morning, Christian opened his door to find a **pale envelope waiting on the threshold.**

His name was typed neatly on the front, but his hands trembled as he picked it up.

He already knew what it contained before he unfolded it.

He had been **conscripted into military service.**

The house of Piguet, the sketches, the delicate folds of silk and lace **—all of it would have to wait.**

Within weeks, Christian had **traded his tailor's chalk for a rifle, his atelier for the barren fields of the French countryside.**

The uniform was stiff, ill-fitting. The boots rubbed blisters into his heels. But what struck him most was **the silence.**

War, he quickly learned, was not the kind he had read about in books. **There were no grand speeches, no noble moments of heroism.**

It was **waiting.**

Hours of **monotony and cold, of staring across an open field and seeing nothing but the wind shifting the grass.** Days of digging trenches, of tightening his belt another notch as food rations dwindled.

And then, **bursts of chaos.**

Gunfire tearing through the stillness. The sharp, acrid smell of burning. The deafening sound of explosions that left the earth shaking beneath him.

Men wrote letters home. Some smoked, their fingers shaking, pretending not to notice the way death lurked just beyond the horizon.

And Christian?

He sketched.

Not landscapes. **Not war. Not soldiers.**

Dresses.

He **drew in the margins of military forms**, on scraps of paper, on the backs of envelopes. He drew silhouettes that had no place in the world he now inhabited—**gowns that swept the floor, cinched waists, delicate folds of fabric that would never touch the mud and blood around him.**

It made no sense.

And yet, **it was the only thing that kept him sane.**

He realized something in those dark, endless nights: **beauty was his only weapon against the war.**

In **1942**, Christian Dior returned to Paris.

But **the city was not the same.**

The Germans were there now. **Their presence was everywhere—marching through the streets, seated in the cafés where once only Parisians had gathered.**

The air was **thick with tension,** a quiet resistance humming beneath every glance, every hurried whisper.

And yet, fashion had not died.

Christian found work at **Lucien Lelong's fashion house**, one of the few that had managed to stay open despite the occupation.

Lelong understood something the Germans did not—**fashion was not just an industry, it was a form of defiance.**

The world may have been at war, but **women still wanted beauty.** And as fabric became scarce, as rations tightened, **designers had to be clever.**

Christian learned how to **create with less**—how to drape a gown using the barest amount of material, how to make something feel luxurious even when opulence was forbidden.

It was a skill he would carry with him for the rest of his life.

But still, **something felt incomplete.**

And so, he turned to fate.

Christian had always believed in **signs, in omens, in the idea that destiny was not something stumbled upon, but something already written, waiting to be revealed.**

He began to seek out **the fortune tellers of Paris.**

They were tucked away in the corners of the city, behind **heavy curtains and doorways marked only by cryptic symbols.**

One night, in a candlelit room filled with the scent of burning incense, **he sat across from an old woman whose eyes were like glass, unreadable.**

She **traced a slow, deliberate circle on the wooden table between them.**

"You will dress women in a way they have never been dressed before," she said, her voice low and certain.

Christian felt a shiver **crawl up his spine.**

"Will I be successful?" he asked. His voice was barely a whisper.

The woman smiled.

"More than you can imagine."

The words settled inside him like a stone sinking to the bottom of a river.

The war was not over. **The world was still crumbling.** But somewhere, beyond all of it, **his future was waiting.**

And soon, **he would meet it.**

One evening, **Christian sat by the Seine, as he often did when his thoughts grew too loud.**

The water reflected the golden glow of the streetlamps, **shimmering like silk against the night sky.**

He reached into his coat pocket and pulled out **his sketchbook.**

He did not draw **a landscape, nor a soldier, nor a city rebuilding itself from ruin.**

He drew a dress.

Something unlike anything he had seen before—**soft yet structured, bold yet elegant.**

It was **a silhouette that whispered of something new, something that did not yet exist, but would.**

And for the first time, **he saw his path clearly.**

He did not yet know that in just a few short years, **the world would know his name.**

He did not yet know that he would **redefine fashion itself, bring femininity back into the war-ravaged world, create something that would outlast him.**

All he knew was that, despite everything—**despite the war, despite the hunger, despite the darkness—he had finally found his way back to beauty.**

And for now, **that was enough.**

Shadows of War and Family Ties

Christian had always known his sister was **braver than most.**

She had a quiet strength, **the kind that didn't boast, didn't seek attention—but simply endured.** She had never been one for frivolous things. While Christian had chased art, spent his nights in salons debating the nature of beauty, Catherine had **observed the world as it was, not as it ought to be.**

So, when war came, when Paris became a city of **hushed voices and lowered eyes**, Catherine did not hesitate.

She joined the **Resistance** without fanfare, without seeking permission.

While Christian sketched gowns and draped silk in Lucien Lelong's atelier, his sister was moving through the streets **like a ghost, unnoticed, untraceable.**

She was part of **F2**, an underground network working against the occupation. **She delivered coded messages, smuggled arms, carried information sewn into the seams of her skirts.**

She **risked everything**, not because she wanted to be a hero, but because she could not bear to **stand idly by** while France bled.

Her world was one of **fake names, safe houses, late-night whispers exchanged in the corners of Parisian cafés.** She learned to move through the city without being seen, to measure the weight of a glance, to hear the **unspoken threats in seemingly ordinary conversations.**

And Christian?

He knew. **Of course, he knew.**

But they never spoke of it.

War had turned **ordinary words into weapons, into liabilities.**

Instead, when Catherine came to visit, they drank tea in the kitchen, and **Christian watched her hands.**

They were still **steady, still unshaken**—but thinner now, paler.

Something in her was changing. **Growing sharper, harder, as if the war was carving her into something else.**

She never spoke about **where she had been, what she had done.**

And he never asked.

Because he knew that one day, **the war would ask too much of her.**

And then, one morning in **1944**, she was **gone.**

The news came in fragments, in whispers, in half-spoken horrors.

Catherine had been **taken.**

The Gestapo had raided a safe house. **Someone had talked.**

Christian **felt the world tilt beneath him.**

His sister—the girl who had once woven flowers into his hair when they were children, who had run barefoot through the gardens of Granville—**was now in the hands of men who did not believe in mercy.**

She was taken to **Avenue Foch**, Gestapo headquarters, a place where **people entered but rarely left.**

Christian could barely breathe as he imagined it.

The sterile hallways. The locked doors. The sound of boots against the floor.

And Catherine—**bound, beaten, but unbroken.**

He ran through the streets of Paris, his breath ragged, **his feet barely touching the ground.**

He begged for information. **No one would speak.**

People lowered their eyes, **afraid to be caught knowing too much.**

The silence was **unbearable.**

At night, he lay awake, staring at the ceiling, picturing her in some **dark room,** her wrists raw from restraints, her voice hoarse from refusing to answer their questions.

Catherine, who had fought **without a weapon,** who had carried her country's secrets **in the folds of her skirt.**

And he could do **nothing.**

Nothing.

The helplessness was a weight on his chest, **crushing him, suffocating him.**

Then, after weeks of limbo, **the final blow came.**

She had been deported.

To **Ravensbrück.**

A **concentration camp.**

The words alone **nearly brought him to his knees.**

He had heard of Ravensbrück. **Everyone had.**

It was **a place of no return.**

And yet, Christian refused to believe she was gone.

Christian Dior knew the war was built on **disappearances.**

People vanished. **That was the nature of war, its cruelty—one moment a person was there, the next, they were gone.**

But **Catherine was not one of those people.**

She **couldn't be.**

He refused to believe it.

At night, when Paris was silent but for the distant sounds of war—the occasional siren, the echo of boots against cobblestone, the rustle of rationed paper bags—**he whispered her name into the darkness.**

"Catherine."

A prayer. A promise. A refusal.

Each morning, he awoke with **a pit in his stomach, a fear so consuming it felt like drowning, but he forced himself to breathe.**

There would be a letter today.

Someone would bring news.

Some small proof that **she was still alive, still fighting, still out there somewhere beneath the same sky.**

But the **letters never came.**

His contacts had **nothing to give him but silence and pity.**

"No word."

"Nothing yet."

"Be patient."

He wanted to **tear the words from their mouths,** shake them until they understood—**Catherine didn't have time for patience.**

Still, he **refused to let go.**

To let go meant accepting she was lost, and Christian was not capable of that.

He clung to hope like a man dangling from the edge of a cliff—**fingers bloodied, grip slipping, but refusing to fall.**

Because if she was still fighting, **then so would he.**

Hope, he found, had to be **fed.**

And when the world would not give him answers, he searched for them elsewhere.

It started with a whisper.

"There is a woman."

"She sees things."

"She may know."

Christian had never been a fool, but he had always **believed in signs.**

His mother had once told him that **some things in life could not be explained, only felt.**

And now, he needed something—**anything—to hold on to.

The first time he stepped into a clairvoyant's shop, the air was **thick with incense, heavy with the scent of wax and old books.**

A woman sat behind a round table, her fingers covered in rings that glinted in the dim candlelight.

She looked at him **as if she already knew.**

"You seek someone."

His voice barely made it past his lips.

"My sister."

She did not ask questions.

She shuffled the tarot deck, placed the cards before him.

The **first card**: **The Tower.**

A city crumbling. Fire. Ruin. **Destruction.**

His hands clenched into fists.

The **second card: The Star.**

Light. **Hope.** A sign that **even after devastation, something still remained.**

The woman studied him for a long moment.

"She is not gone," she said. *"She is fighting."*

The words **wrapped around him like armor.**

They became his new reality.

He would not believe in death. **He would believe in fate.**

So he returned.

To her. To others. **To any person who promised to read beyond the veil of this world.**

He became **a man possessed**, searching for signs in places he never would have before, seeking the unseen forces that had always whispered to him.

"She is alive."

"She will return."

Each time, their words **strengthened him.**

Each time, **he walked away knowing he could not stop.**

Because **if fate had already decided, then he had to be ready.**

The silence **began to seep into his work.**

His sketches changed.

They became **something else—something raw, urgent, filled with emotion he could not name but could only express through fabric.**

At night, he sat at his drafting table, surrounded by half-formed designs, the scent of **pencil shavings and candle wax** thick in the air.

For hours, he did nothing.

Because how could he create **beauty in a world that had devoured the only thing that mattered?**

Then, **his hand moved.**

The pencil met the paper, and before he could think, **the lines began to take shape.**

His sketches were **fluid yet structured, softer yet unbreakable—like Catherine.**

Gowns **formed from his grief, from his defiance, from the part of him that refused to let the war steal another thing.**

Each stroke of his pencil was a fight.

Every gown, a rebellion.

His designs were **not just dresses. They were survival.**

Christian **worked until his hands ached.**

Until dawn **spilled pale light onto the fabric draped over his chair.**

Until exhaustion blurred the lines, and his body demanded rest, **but his heart would not let him stop.**

Because **if he stopped—truly stopped—then she really would be gone.**

And **he refused to accept that.**

So he stitched together **hope, grief, and defiance, weaving them into something tangible.**

Something that could not be erased.

Something that would **outlive war.**

Because if the world would not give him Catherine, **he would carve her into something permanent.**

He could not save her.

But he could create something **so beautiful, so enduring, that war itself could not destroy it.**

And that—**that was the only thing keeping him from drowning.**

The Birth of the New Look

P aris was alive again.
At least, that was what people said.
The war had ended. The Nazis were gone. **The city had its streets back, its cafés, its sky—yet it did not feel the same.**

It was a Paris that had learned to live with **hunger, with loss, with waiting.**

The Seine still flowed, but now its waters carried whispers of things that had been stolen: **brothers who never came home, mothers who had disappeared into camps, lovers who had vanished without a goodbye.**

Christian walked these streets, **seeing ghosts everywhere.**

He saw Catherine.

Not in flesh—**not yet**—but in the tilt of a woman's chin, in the way a scarf fluttered behind a stranger's shoulder, in the scent of roses that caught him off guard on a quiet morning.

She had been gone for over a year now.

And still, **he refused to believe she would not return.**

Somewhere, she was **alive.** She had to be.

And so, while others spoke of moving on, **Christian refused to let go.**

But how does a man survive on **faith alone?**

The answer came, unexpectedly, **in fabric.**

Christian had spent the last few years **hiding inside his work.**

Fashion had saved him—**or at least, had given him something to hold onto while he waited.**

He had spent the war at **Lucien Lelong's house**, designing under the constraints of occupation, rationed textiles, and a city that had forgotten what luxury felt like.

But now, the war was over. **And the world needed beauty again.**

So when **Marcel Boussac—the textile magnate, the man they called "The Cotton King"—offered to back him, Christian hesitated.**

Boussac wanted him to take over an existing fashion house, **Philippe et Gaston**, a struggling brand in need of reinvention.

But Christian did not want to **repair the old.**

He wanted to **create something new.**

Something that did not belong to the past, or to the war, or to the men who had once dictated how fashion should look.

Something that belonged only to him.

And so, he took a risk.

"No," he told Boussac. *"I don't want to revive someone else's house. I want to build my own."*

It was a bold demand. **Perhaps reckless.**

But Boussac saw something in Christian's eyes—something **unyielding.**

And so, in 1946, Christian Dior opened the doors to his own fashion house at **30 Avenue Montaigne.**

He had no idea, then, **that he was about to change the world.**

It had started in whispers, in sketches done in the dead of night.

It was **a feeling more than a design**, a longing for something **grander, softer, more human.**

During the war, fashion had been **practical, restrained, stripped of indulgence.** Women had dressed for necessity, not for beauty.

But now, Christian wanted to bring back **the dream.**

He thought of **his mother.**

He thought of **Catherine.**

He thought of **every woman who had suffered, who had waited, who had lost.**

And he thought of **rebirth.**

He imagined **cinched waists, full skirts, fabric that swayed like poetry.**

He imagined **women looking in the mirror and seeing something they had forgotten—elegance, romance, something softer than war.**

And so, he designed.

Not for Paris as it was, but for Paris as it could be.

A city reborn.

A world that remembered how to dream.

That morning, the world did not know that it was about to change.

The small salon at **30 Avenue Montaigne** filled with **editors, socialites, buyers—each of them expectant, but unaware.**

Christian stood behind the heavy curtains, **his heart pounding.**

He had never been a nervous man.

But today, **everything was at stake.**

He thought of **Catherine.**

Where was she now?

Was she alive?

Would she ever know what he had built in her absence?

The room fell silent as **the first model stepped onto the runway.**

Gasps rippled through the audience.

The first gown—a jacket nipped at the waist, a skirt that **swelled like a blooming flower**—moved through the room like a revolution.

Then another. And another.

Fabric cascaded in soft waves. **Hems dropped to the mid-calf, a** rebellion against the boxy, wartime silhouettes that had ruled for so long.

The models walked with **grace, with presence, with the confidence of a world that was daring to hope again.**

And then, the applause.

It was thunderous, rapturous—**something between astonishment and relief.**

Women wept.

"This is what we have been waiting for," one of them whispered.

And just like that, fashion was reborn.

The world would call it **The New Look.**

But for Christian, it was more than that.

It was **a return to softness, to beauty, to life itself.**

And in the chaos of applause, in the flashes of cameras, in the rush of voices that swelled around him—**Christian felt the weight of war finally lift from his chest.**

For the first time in years, **he allowed himself to believe.**

Catherine would return.

She had to.

Because the world had made room for beauty again.

And **Catherine was the most beautiful thing he had ever known.**

The next morning, the newspapers did not simply review his collection.

They crowned him.

"Christian Dior rescues fashion from its post-war gloom."

"Paris has remembered how to dream."

"A revolution in femininity: Dior's 'New Look' changes everything."

Overnight, he became **not just a designer, but a legend.**

Orders poured in. Women flocked to his boutique, desperate for gowns that made them feel **alive again.**

But beneath the success, beneath the celebrations and champagne toasts, **Christian waited.**

Waited for the letter, for the phone call, for the knock on the door.

Waited for **Catherine.**

She had survived war.

Now, she had to survive **the aftermath.**

And when she finally returned—when she walked through the doors of 30 Avenue Montaigne—**he would be ready.**

He would **clothe her in beauty, in victory, in everything war had tried to steal from them both.**

Until then, he would keep designing.

Keep hoping.

Keep waiting.

Because **the world had been reborn.**

And so, too, would she.

Fragrance of Memories

The applause from the **New Look** still echoed in his ears.

Paris had embraced his vision, the world had declared him a genius, and yet, Christian Dior felt **unsettled.**

Something was missing.

He had restored beauty to the world, had given women back their elegance, their softness, their place in the light. But there was a **void inside him that fashion alone could not fill.**

His gowns moved like poetry, his designs celebrated rebirth, but there was something more he wanted to capture—**something invisible, something untouchable, yet deeply felt.**

Something like a memory.

Something like **Catherine.**

She had returned, **thin, quiet, haunted, but alive.**

Yet, she did not speak of **Ravensbrück.**

She did not share the horrors she had endured.

And Christian, though desperate to know, **never asked.**

Instead, he watched her from across the room as she moved **like a shadow of herself**, as if part of her was still trapped in the places she had barely escaped.

He wanted to give her something back.

Something **untouched by war.**
Something from **before.**
And that was when he knew.
Fashion was not enough.
If he could not protect her from the past, he would bottle it instead.
He would give her something that would never fade.
Something that smelled like **home.**

Before the war.

Before the hunger and the waiting and the terror of missing people and missing years.

Before Paris, before fashion, before success—**there had been Granville.**

Their childhood home, perched high on the cliffs of Normandy, where the sea wind mixed with **the scent of roses from their mother's garden.**

The garden had been **Madeleine Dior's masterpiece**, her pride.

Soft pink and white roses, bursting in full bloom, jasmine curling around iron gates, gardenias thriving in the shade.

A place untouched by time, by sorrow, by war.

Christian and Catherine had spent their childhood there, running barefoot through the damp grass, **their laughter rising like birds into the summer air.**

Their mother would scold them for **bruising the petals**, but Catherine would pluck them anyway, rubbing them between her small fingers until their scent clung to her skin.

"We'll always have this," she had whispered to him once, **cupping a rose in her hands like a secret.**

"Even when we're older. Even when we leave."

But the garden had not followed them.

War had stolen it.

War had stolen **so much.**

And yet, the scent—the **memory of it**—had never left him.

It was still there, **locked inside him,** waiting to be brought back to life.

And now, it was time.

Christian had always believed that **perfume was more than a fragrance.**

It was **a signature, an extension of identity, an intimate whisper left behind in a room long after a woman had gone.**

But now, **it was something else.**

It was **a way to reclaim the past.**

A way to bring Catherine back to **who she was before the war had touched her.**

He wanted to create a scent that **felt like childhood, like home, like survival.**

Something bright, yet delicate. Romantic, yet **unbreakable.**

Something that would smell like Catherine.

But how does one **capture a memory?**

It had to be **roses**, of course.

Their mother's roses.

But not just roses—**there had to be something more.**

A touch of **jasmine, the way it used to cling to the garden walls at night.**

A note of **gardenia, rich and creamy, just as their mother had worn in her perfume.**

A fragrance that carried **not just beauty, but strength.**

A scent that **did not bow to war, but bloomed despite it.**

The perfumers came, **masters of their craft,** their hands familiar with the delicate balance of essences and oils.

They mixed.

They blended.

They searched for the scent that **Christian could already smell in his memory.**

But nothing was right.

Not yet.

The first batch was **too sweet.**

The second, **too heavy.**

He sat for hours, leaning over glass bottles, inhaling deeply, **closing his eyes and waiting.**

He thought of Granville.

He thought of **the roses.**

He thought of **Catherine, standing in the garden, twirling in the soft summer breeze, before war, before suffering.**

Then—finally—there it was.

The scent **wrapped around him like a forgotten lullaby.**

Soft, elegant, wild, and alive.

It **was her.**

It was **everything they had lost, and everything that had survived.**

And now, it would live forever.

One evening, Christian sat in his atelier, **finalizing the scent**, the small glass bottle sitting in front of him like a treasure.

But it still had no name.

And then—**a voice.**

"Ah, here comes Miss Dior."

Mitzah Bricard, his muse, his ever-dramatic, ever-elegant confidante, had turned toward the doorway, her eyes lighting up as Catherine entered the room.

Thin. Weary. **But alive.**

Christian's breath caught in his throat.

And just like that, **the name was born.**

It **wasn't just a perfume anymore.**

It was **Catherine.**

It was **a tribute, a promise, a love letter.**

Miss Dior.

The scent of survival.

The scent of **everything that had endured.**

. . .

When Miss Dior was finally bottled, **Christian held it in his hands, running his fingers over the delicate glass.**

It was **more than perfume.**

It was **a memory, preserved in scent.**

A piece of their childhood, **bottled before time could steal it away.**

It was **resilience.**

It was **remembrance.**

It was **Catherine.**

The first bottles left **30 Avenue Montaigne**, carried away by women who dabbed the scent onto their wrists, their throats, letting it sink into their skin like a whisper of something **forgotten but never truly lost.**

Just like Catherine.

Just like the garden in Granville.

Just like the past that had shaped them both—**woven into fragrance, unshakable, immortal.**

And as Christian watched the world embrace Miss Dior, he knew—**even if the roses wilted, even if the war had changed them all, some things would last forever.**

And Miss Dior would be one of them.

Blossoming into an Empire

The streets of Paris were coming alive again.

The war had left the city **fractured, haunted, and worn thin**, but now, **it was stitching itself back together**, piece by piece, like the delicate fabrics that passed through Christian Dior's fingers.

His empire was taking root. **A world he had built from the ashes of war, from longing, from memory.**

Women swirled in **silk skirts and cinched waists**, stepping into the future with the grace they had once been forced to abandon. The New Look was no longer a trend—it was **a movement.**

Orders flooded in from **New York, Rome, London.** His fashion house was no longer just a Parisian secret—**it was a global obsession.**

And yet, no matter how high he climbed, **his heart remained tethered to the past.**

Some mornings, he would wake before dawn and stand by his window, watching as the streets stirred awake. He would close his eyes and inhale the cool morning air, **half-expecting to smell the roses of Granville, the sea breeze of home, the childhood he and Catherine had once shared.**

But Paris had a different scent now.

It smelled of **freshly baked bread, of cobblestone after rain, of perfume lingering in the air like a promise.**

And still, somewhere beneath it all, **he swore he could smell Catherine's absence.**

Dior fever swept across the world.

American women, once accustomed to **stiff, rationed wartime clothing**, suddenly demanded dresses that swayed when they walked, that whispered luxury, that **made them feel beautiful again.**

Christian barely had time to breathe.

His designs graced **the pages of Vogue, the bodies of Hollywood stars, the halls of royalty.**

At night, he sat in his office at **30 Avenue Montaigne**, surrounded by letters and telegrams from across the world.

"We need more orders shipped to New York immediately."

"Princess Margaret is requesting a private fitting."

"The Americans say Paris belongs to Dior now."

It was intoxicating. It was overwhelming.

It was **everything he had dreamed of.**

And yet, amidst the champagne toasts and the flashes of cameras, **he would sometimes look up and find himself lost.**

Lost in the faces of the women he dressed.

Lost in the noise of the world that had crowned him king of couture.

Because for all the beauty he had created, **one face was still missing.**

One voice still absent from the chorus.

And every so often, when the scent of roses drifted unexpectedly through the air, **his heart ached in ways success could never soothe.**

Catherine visited him at the atelier sometimes, stepping softly into his world like a shadow moving through silk.

She would walk between the racks of gowns, **running her fingers along the fabric, her touch light, hesitant.**

A Parisian Fairytale: Christiaan Dior's Journey fr... 39

And Christian would watch her, wondering **how much of her had been left behind in Ravensbrück.**

She never spoke of it.

Not of the pain, not of the hunger, not of the months in captivity that had taken **something from her that he would never be able to restore.**

But he saw it in the way she **sometimes flinched at loud noises, in the way her hands curled into fists when she thought no one was looking.**

And Christian—**who had built an empire in her absence, who had dressed women in silk and dreams while she had been suffering in silence**—felt the guilt like a weight in his chest.

He had waited for her.

Had **believed, against all logic, that she would return.**

But he had not saved her.

When the war had taken her, he had been helpless. **Just a man with a pencil and fabric, designing beauty while she fought for her life.**

And now, as he watched her stand in his world of satin and pearls, he wondered—**was it enough?**

Had he done enough?

She had survived.

But had she truly come back?

Christian was surrounded by people, but **he was always a little bit alone.**

The world **worshiped him**, yet he never let them too close.

He loved his work. He loved his fabrics, his sketches, the quiet magic of an empty atelier in the early morning light.

But at night, when the parties were over, when the champagne had stopped flowing, **he was alone with his thoughts.**

And so, he turned to **the things that had always given him comfort.**

Superstition. Fate. The unseen.

He consulted **his clairvoyants** before major decisions.

He **refused to begin a collection** without first seeking an omen.

He carried **a lucky star in his pocket, a reminder that some forces in life were beyond control.**

And maybe that's why he still saw Catherine everywhere.

In the curve of a model's smile.

In the softness of a white rose placed on his desk.

In the flickering candle at the end of a long evening, when he swore he felt the ghosts of the past pressing against his skin.

He lived in a world of silk and shadows.

But **some ghosts never left.**

By 1950, **Dior was no longer a name—it was a dynasty.**

He had expanded beyond dresses.

Now, there were **handbags, shoes, jewelry—a whole world shaped in his vision, a world where women could drape themselves in Dior and feel like they had stepped into something enchanted.**

The House of Dior stood **at the center of the fashion universe,** its influence stretching across continents.

Christian should have been content.

But **he knew better than anyone that beauty was fleeting.**

He knew that **nothing in life was permanent.**

He had seen the world burn and rebuild itself.

He had watched his sister **disappear into war and return a stranger to herself.**

He had spent his life chasing beauty, trying to catch something that **could not be held.**

So he worked harder.

He designed faster.

He reached for more.

Because deep down, **he was still that boy in Granville, running through his mother's rose garden with Catherine, believing—just for a moment—that time could stand still.**

And if he worked hard enough, if he built something **so exquisite, so untouchable, so eternal,**

Maybe—just maybe—**it finally would.**

The Ghost at the Door

The war had ended. The world had **moved on.**
    The streets of Paris bustled once more with the rhythm of life—**women in cinched waists, their heels clicking on cobblestone, café chairs filled with voices rising above clinking glasses, the scent of Miss Dior lingering in the air.**

Christian Dior had done it.

He had built **an empire out of dreams, out of memory, out of longing.**

And yet, for all the beauty that surrounded him, **he was still waiting.**

Waiting for the knock at the door that would change everything.

Waiting for **his sister.**

The telegram arrived first.

It was brief. **Too brief.**

"She is alive."

Two words. Nothing more.

Christian sat with the paper clenched in his hands, staring at the ink as if by sheer force of will he could pull more meaning from the letters.

He had imagined this moment so many times.

In his mind, it had always been **dramatic, cinematic—a sudden reunion on the steps of 30 Avenue Montaigne, an embrace that erased time and suffering.**

But reality was never like the movies.

Reality was **quieter.**

Reality was a **thin figure stepping off a train at the Gare de l'Est**, wrapped in an oversized coat that swallowed her whole, her dark eyes scanning the platform, looking for something—**or someone.**

Christian saw her before she saw him.

And for a moment, **he couldn't move.**

This was **not the Catherine he remembered.**

The Catherine who had once danced through their mother's rose garden in Granville, who had teased him for his superstitions, who had run through Paris with **fire in her veins and the Resistance in her blood.**

This Catherine was **smaller.**

Her cheekbones were sharp, her skin stretched thin over them. **Her hands, once so full of life, were trembling as she clutched a small, battered bag to her chest.**

Then, her eyes met his.

For a breath, they just stood there.

Two ghosts of the past, staring at one another, measuring the distance between what they had been and **what war had turned them into.**

Then, finally—**movement.**

Christian **rushed to her, gathering her in his arms before she could disappear again.**

"*Catherine,*" he whispered into her shoulder, his voice breaking, "*you came back.*"

She didn't cry.

Neither did he.

They just stood there, holding onto each other **as if time had stopped, as if war had not stolen years from them, as if they could keep this moment forever.**

But even as Christian held her, **he knew the truth.**

The war had taken **more than just time.**

And the sister he had lost—**she was not the same one who had come home.**

The first few nights back in Paris, **Catherine barely spoke.**

Christian brought her to his apartment—**a space filled with soft fabrics, elegant furniture, the warmth of something untouched by war.**

She sat in his armchair, wrapped in a blanket, her hands curled around a cup of tea.

She sipped it **slowly, mechanically, as if drinking was something she had to remind herself to do.**

He tried to fill the silence.

He told her about the world, about how Paris had changed. **About Miss Dior. About the fashion house.**

He tried to make her smile.

But Catherine sat **as still as a statue**, her fingers tightening around the porcelain, as if afraid to let it go.

Christian knew she was **there, physically.**

But her mind?

Her mind was still in Ravensbrück.

The Paris that Christian lived in—the one of **fashion shows and champagne, of women rediscovering silk and laughter—felt foreign to her.**

The war had **left its mark on the city**, but Catherine had been to places that had stripped a person of everything they were.

She walked through the streets as if she were still **a prisoner in an invisible cage.**

Crowds made her nervous.

The sudden sound of **a door slamming, a car backfiring, the shuffling of uniformed men in the distance—all of it made her flinch.**

And yet, she did not complain.

She did not cry.

She did not rage.

She **just endured.**

One evening, Christian took her to dinner at **Maxim's**, a restaurant that had once been a haunt for Resistance members before the war.

The moment they stepped inside, a waiter **recognized her.**

"Mademoiselle Dior," he said, his voice kind but cautious, *"it is... good to see you again."*

Catherine **stiffened.**

Not because of the words—**but because of the way the other diners had turned to look at her.**

They knew.

Everyone knew.

What she had been through. Where she had been.

The way **some of them lowered their eyes in shame, while others stared in curiosity or pity, was unbearable.**

She lasted **less than five minutes.**

Christian followed her outside, **finding her pressed against the stone wall of the building, her breath uneven, her hands clenched into fists.**

"I don't belong here," she whispered, more to herself than to him.

"Catherine—"

"I don't belong anywhere."

Christian had **never hated war more than he did in that moment.**

It had taken so much from them. **And even after it was over, it refused to let them go.**

Christian had **spent the war waiting.**

Waiting for letters.

Waiting for news.

Waiting for a miracle.

And now that Catherine was here, **he did not know how to reach her.**

He brought her to the **House of Dior**, hoping the elegance, the beauty, the movement of it all would remind her that the world still had wonderful things to offer.

She watched as models twirled in front of mirrors, as seamstresses worked tirelessly on gowns, as fabric whispered against skin like poetry.

But she stood in the corner, **silent.**

Christian walked up to her, his voice gentle.

"What do you think?"

She was quiet for a long time.

Then she shook her head.

"I don't belong in this world."

Christian's heart broke.

Because **he had built this world for her.**

For beauty.

For survival.

For a life where **elegance could defy destruction.**

But Catherine did not want to live in **a world of silk and couture.**

She needed something simpler.

Something real.

It happened one morning.

Christian had stepped outside into the **courtyard of Avenue Montaigne**, the early light filtering softly through the iron gates.

And there, standing before a **single white rose blooming in a terracotta pot**, was Catherine.

She reached out, **her fingers brushing the petals.**

A moment of stillness.

A single breath.

Then, she **sank to her knees, her shoulders trembling.**

And for the first time since she had come home—**she cried.**

Christian **stood frozen.**

The sister who had survived **Ravensbrück, the interrogations, the pain—the sister who had not broken, not once—was crying.**

And suddenly, he was a child again, standing in their mother's rose garden, watching her pick petals and press them to her skin.

He swallowed against the lump in his throat, then knelt beside her.

He didn't say anything.

He simply **held her hand.**

Because **sometimes, the only thing you could do for someone who had been through hell was to remind them they weren't alone.**

And as the scent of the rose filled the air, Christian Dior made a silent promise:

That no matter where she went from here—**she would always have a place to return to.**

Catherine never spoke much about what she endured at **Ravensbrück.**

Christian had tried, gently, to ask in the beginning. **Did she have enough food? Did they hurt you? Did you think you would make it out?**

But each time, she would either give him **a thin, tired smile** or a simple, quiet answer that told him **she would never truly share what had happened there.**

She had survived.

That was all she allowed him to know.

And so, instead of pressing her, he watched her. **Waited for signs of what she needed.**

At first, she drifted between places. **His apartment. A friend's home. A borrowed room.**

But she was restless. **She did not belong in the world of couture, of lavish dinners and whispered conversations about hemlines.**

Christian saw it in the way she shifted uncomfortably during fittings, in the way she avoided the extravagant parties he was now expected to attend.

She was looking for **something simpler, something real.**

Then, one morning, he found her at **the flower markets of Les Halles.**

It was **early—before dawn, before Paris had fully woken up.** The stalls were lined with crates of fresh-cut flowers, vendors haggling with café owners and socialites looking for the perfect bouquet.

And there, in the midst of it all, was Catherine.

She was speaking with an old flower merchant, **her fingers trailing absentmindedly over the petals of a bundle of lavender.**

Christian stood back, watching.

She looked more alive here than she had in weeks.

She was not the Catherine who had danced through their mother's rose garden as a child, nor the fierce Resistance fighter he had lost to war.

But she was **someone new.**

Someone healing.

Days later, she told him **she had found work at the flower market.**

"I like it," she said simply, arranging a bouquet as they sat together in his apartment.

"The mornings are peaceful. The people are kind."

Christian knew what she meant.

Here, surrounded by flowers, **there were no questions. No past. No expectations.**

Just **beauty. Simplicity. Life.**

And so, he did not question her decision.

Instead, he kissed her forehead and whispered, *"Then I'm happy for you, Catherine."*

Because **if she had found a way to move forward, so could he.**

Even as she built her new life among flowers, **Catherine never truly left Christian's world.**

She was there in **his sketches, in his perfume, in the way he spoke about resilience and beauty as if they were the same thing.**

She was in the **delicate curves of the gowns he designed**, in the way he draped fabric so it flowed like a memory that could never be erased.

She was in the perfume bottles of **Miss Dior**, sitting on vanities across the world, carrying the scent of **roses, gardenia, jasmine— Granville, childhood, survival.**

She was in the name people whispered as they passed through the House of Dior:

"Miss Dior."

She did not want the spotlight. **She had seen too much of the world to crave attention.**

But Christian made sure **she would never be forgotten.**

And sometimes, when he walked past her flower stall in the early morning and saw her hands busy tying a silk ribbon around a bouquet, he would smile.

Because even though they had found **different paths, different ways to survive,** they had made it here.

Together.

And **that was enough.**

One evening, **just as the sun was setting**, Catherine sat beside Christian in the courtyard of **30 Avenue Montaigne.**

The city was quiet in that rare, golden moment before night fully took hold.

Catherine leaned back against the garden bench, **tilting her head toward the sky, breathing in the scent of roses from the potted plants.**

"I think of Granville sometimes," she said softly.

Christian's chest tightened.

"I do too," he admitted.

She turned to look at him.

"Do you ever miss it?"

Christian swallowed. **Of course, he missed it.**

The house on the cliffs, their mother's garden, the afternoons spent beneath the warm Normandy sun, Catherine **spinning through the grass with roses clutched in her small hands.**

But **they could not go back.**

And so, he shook his head.

"Not in the way I used to."

Catherine studied him for a long moment, then nodded, as if she understood something unspoken.

Then she smiled—**small, quiet, but real.**

And in that moment, Christian made a promise.

That everything he built, everything he created, **would carry their past with it, woven into silk and scent, into whispers of elegance and memory.**

That as long as Dior existed, **so would Catherine.**

So would **Granville.**

So would **the roses.**

The world of Dior was **expanding.**

The House of Dior was no longer just a name—it was **an empire, stretching beyond the borders of France, beyond the boundaries of fashion itself.**

But even as Christian stood on the cusp of something **even greater**, he never lost sight of why he had begun.

Fashion was not just **fabric** to him.

It was **architecture.** It was **storytelling.** It was **memory woven into shape and silhouette.**

And as he designed his next collection, he thought not just of the women who would wear it, but of **the women who had shaped him.**

His mother, who had taught him that beauty was a form of grace.

Catherine, who had taught him that survival was its own kind of elegance.

And as he laid the first sketches onto his desk, **he smiled.**

Because this was not just a fashion house.

This was **a house built on love.**

A house **where Catherine's name would never be forgotten.**

And a house that, **even long after he was gone, would carry their story forward—stitched into every seam, sewn into every dream.**

The Architect and the Man Behind Dior

Christian Dior was not just a designer.
He was **a builder, a sculptor, an architect of fabric and form.**
To the world, a dress was something worn, something functional—**but to Dior, it was a structure, a carefully calculated composition, as deliberate as the grand palaces of Paris.**

A gown could hold **space**, just like a columned façade, its folds and layers engineered to stand **not just with beauty, but with purpose.**

He had long been **fascinated by form and proportion**—not just in fashion, but in everything around him.

As a boy, he had wandered the gardens of **Granville**, studying the way his mother's roses bloomed in perfect symmetry, each petal unfurling with a natural elegance that seemed preordained.

Later, in Paris, he marveled at **Haussmann's boulevards**—the sweeping streets, the way light bounced off the limestone façades, how the city had been carefully reshaped to exude grandeur and order.

And when he began designing, he **applied that same philosophy to fashion.**

A dress was not just a dress.

It was a **structure**, a study in line and balance, proportion and contrast.

Dior did not simply sketch an idea and hand it off to his seamstresses.

He worked **with them, alongside them, obsessing over every pleat, every fold, every millimeter of fabric that touched the body.**

In his ateliers, muslin toile became his blueprint, the dress form **his canvas, his building frame.**

He would stand, pinning fabric to a mannequin, watching how it curved, how it reacted to movement, how it captured light.

A gown, he believed, **must have a foundation—an internal structure that held everything in place, invisible to the eye but essential to the silhouette.**

The waist was **the keystone**, the central point from which everything radiated.

The bust and shoulders were **the framework**, requiring support, balance, tension.

And the skirt—ah, the skirt—**it was the grand façade, the theatrical statement, the part of the garment that moved with the body, revealing its life and energy.**

Dior's favorite silhouette—the **cinched waist, the full skirt—was not a coincidence.**

It was an architectural marvel, a direct rebellion against the straight, austere lines of wartime fashion.

He wanted women to have **volume again, movement again, presence again.**

He built his dresses **the way a cathedral is built**—with careful scaffolding beneath the surface, invisible but integral.

Corsetry returned, not as a means of restriction, but as a way to create **a perfect, sculpted shape.**

Petticoats were layered **like the foundation stones of a monument, creating grandeur from the inside out.**

Every dart, every seam, every hidden panel was placed **with intention**, designed not just for beauty, but for structure, for strength.

. . .

Dior was not an artist who worked alone.

Like an architect with his masons, like a sculptor with his stonecutters, he surrounded himself with **masters of their craft.**

Tailors, drapers, pattern-makers—each had a hand in shaping his vision, bringing his designs from paper to reality.

He listened to them, watched how their hands moved, how they shaped fabric with the same precision that a sculptor carved marble.

When a design was not quite right, he did not simply say, **"Fix it."**

He stood beside them, **adjusting, pinning, testing.**

He studied the cut of a bodice the way a structural engineer studies the weight distribution of a bridge.

The women who wore his gowns were not just wearing fabric.

They were **walking in a carefully engineered creation, a piece of architecture made of silk and thread.**

And like the grandest buildings in Paris, **his work was built to last.**

Timeless.

Unshakable.

A legacy that would stand long after he was gone.

Fashion was not just **clothing** to Christian.

It was **a performance.**

A dress was not simply stitched—it was **composed, like a symphony, each seam a note, each fabric a melody.**

His shows were not **ordinary runway presentations.**

They were **orchestrated, staged like grand productions, as dramatic as the opera, as carefully designed as the architecture of Paris itself.**

From the moment the first model stepped forward, **a Dior show was a world unto itself.**

The room fell silent, anticipation hanging in the air like perfume.

Then, **the music swelled.**

Strings, soft at first, then fuller, richer, carrying the weight of expectation.

A flicker of light, illuminating a single gown—the shimmer of silk catching the glow like moonlight on water.

And then, she moved.

The model glided, her gown **not just worn, but performed.**

The cinched waist, the full skirt—**they did not simply exist, they told a story.**

Each step, each turn, was a whisper of a different era, a love letter to femininity, a rebirth of something the war had tried to take away.

Dior understood the power of **the moment.**

A woman did not simply step into his designs—**she stepped into a fantasy.**

She became **part of the world he had created, a world where elegance reigned and beauty was not a luxury but a necessity.**

When the show ended, when the last gown had vanished behind the curtains, there was always a pause—**a breathless silence before the applause erupted.**

And Christian stood there, in the shadows of the grand salons, watching, knowing.

This was not just fashion.

This was a **dream, made real.**

To the world, Christian Dior was a **visionary, a master of elegance, a king of couture.**

His name shimmered in the pages of **Vogue**, was whispered in the corridors of high society, was etched onto the delicate labels of gowns that women dreamed of wearing.

But behind the brilliance, behind the flashing cameras and the endless fittings, **Christian longed for quiet.**

He had never been a man who thrived in crowds.

The salons of Paris—filled with chatter, with swirling cigarette smoke, with the electricity of ambition—**exhausted him.**

The grand parties, the glittering nights at Maxim's, the private fittings with royalty—**he attended, but never belonged.**

What he craved, what he **truly loved**, was something far simpler.

He found it in the countryside, in the stillness of **his home in Milly-la-Forêt**, far from the marble halls of Avenue Montaigne.

There, away from the weight of expectation, he was **just Christian**.

No sketches to approve. No buyers to impress. No critics to please.

Just **him, his garden, and the rhythm of nature.**

He walked among the flowers, touching the petals with the same reverence he gave to silk.

He knelt in the damp earth, dirt clinging to his fingers, the scent of lavender and rosemary rising in the early morning air.

Here, in the quiet, he was no longer **the man who had built an empire, the man who had dressed queens and film stars.**

He was the boy from Granville.

The boy who had wandered through **his mother's rose garden**, entranced by the way light kissed the edges of petals.

The boy who had once watched Catherine weave flowers into her hair, laughing, carefree.

Perhaps, deep down, **he had never really left that garden.**

Paris was his stage. **But nature was his sanctuary.**

He disliked interviews, the endless questions, the reporters who tried to pry beyond his perfectly tailored image.

"My work speaks for itself," he would say with a smile, neatly dodging the hunger for scandal, for gossip.

Let them talk about **the dresses, the perfume, the dream he had created.**

But Christian Dior?

The man, the dreamer, the artist?

That part of him would remain untouched.

Christian had always believed in **signs, in fate, in the things that could not be explained.**

He was a man of fabric and form, of craftsmanship and precision, yet **he never ignored the unseen forces that moved the world.**

In his pocket, he carried **a lucky star—just a small charm, unremarkable to anyone else, but to him, it was everything.**

He consulted **clairvoyants before major decisions, listened carefully to omens.**

Some thought it **eccentric**—a touch of whimsy in a man of great intellect.

But Christian knew better.

He had seen too much in his life to dismiss the mysteries of the universe.

And then came **the tarot reading.**

It had been a simple encounter, no different from the others he had sought out over the years.

The cards were shuffled, laid out before him.

The fortune-teller studied them, eyes flickering with something she tried to mask.

"You will not grow old."

Christian **laughed.**

A nervous chuckle, a polite dismissal.

"Then I must work quickly," he said, pushing aside the warning with **his usual grace, his usual charm.**

But later that night, when the candles in his room flickered in the silence, **the words remained.**

They clung to the edges of his thoughts, quiet but insistent.

Fate had always been kind to him. **Hadn't it?**

It had given him **talent, success, adoration.**

It had **spared Catherine, brought her back to him.**

Surely, fate would not **betray him now.**

And yet, in the stillness, in the quiet corners of his mind, **he could not quite shake the fear that time was slipping through his fingers.**

Christian Dior was a **paradox.**

He was **a romantic**, a man who built gowns as though they were poetry, who believed in elegance as a philosophy, who understood that fashion was more than just clothing—it was **a way of life.**

But he was also **a businessman.**

His empire did not thrive on sentiment alone.

He **knew the numbers, the strategies, the ruthless mechanics of the industry.**

While others lost themselves in the fantasy, he remained **grounded in reality.**

He understood that behind the sweeping skirts and delicate embroidery, there had to be **structure, discipline, control.**

It was this **duality** that made Dior **irresistible.**

Women fell in love with the **romance of his designs, the dream of stepping into a world of grace and refinement.**

But behind the dream, **there was steel.**

A relentless pursuit of **perfection.**

An understanding that fashion was not just **art—it was business.**

And business, like beauty, had to be carefully constructed.

His empire had reached its **peak.**

Dior was no longer just a name.

It was a legend.

The House of Dior had expanded beyond anything he had imagined—**gowns, perfumes, accessories, a world built in his image.**

But **legends, like dreams, are fragile things.**

And though Christian had built **a house of beauty, a fortress of fashion, a kingdom made of silk and ambition,**

He could not escape the whispers of fate that followed him like shadows.

Legacy of Elegance

In the autumn of 1957, Christian Dior retreated to **Montecatini, Italy**, seeking rest, seeking stillness.

The weight of his empire had grown heavy. **His name was now larger than himself, sewn into the labels of dresses worn by queens, socialites, and Hollywood stars.**

But even legends needed to breathe.

He had been feeling **tired**, though he told few people. He was only fifty-two—**there was still so much left to do, so many designs he had yet to create.**

Still, he had learned to listen to the quiet warnings in his heart.

Hadn't he always believed in fate?

Hadn't the cards once whispered of **an untimely end**?

He had laughed it off, but the thought had **never truly left him**.

In Italy, the days were warm, the air scented with citrus and the salt of the sea.

Perhaps this was the **pause** he needed before the next chapter of Dior.

But the next chapter would never come.

On October 24, 1957, Christian Dior suffered a fatal heart attack.

The world fell silent.

Paris, the city he had stitched back to life with silk and dreams, **mourned.**

The House of Dior—**his House, his vision, his life's work—was left without its creator.**

The man who had revived elegance, who had given women back their beauty, was **gone.**

For a moment, there was **uncertainty.**

Could Dior exist without **Christian Dior?**

His name was sewn into gowns, whispered in salons, painted across glossy magazines.

But it was **his hands, his mind, his instincts that had built it all.**

Without him, would it all **crumble?**

But Christian had always been a man of **structure.**

Just as an architect designs a cathedral to stand **long after he is gone**, he had built the House of Dior to endure.

And so, his empire **continued.**

A young man—**only 21 years old—stepped into the role Dior had left behind.**

His name was **Yves Saint Laurent.**

Dior had seen something in him, had nurtured him, had whispered to those closest to him that this boy might one day **shape the future.**

And so, **he did.**

The world did not forget Dior.

It **wore him, loved him, carried him forward.**

Of all those who grieved, **Catherine grieved the deepest.**

She had **fought wars.**

She had survived **Ravensbrück, interrogation, starvation.**

She had lost so much, had seen the worst of humanity.

And yet, it was **this loss**—the loss of **her brother, the one** constant in her life, the man who had built something beautiful in the wake of destruction—that nearly broke her.

But Catherine **did not let grief consume her.**

Instead, she made it her **mission** to ensure that Christian's legacy remained **untouched, unforgotten.**

She became the **guardian of his memory**, dedicating herself to preserving **his work, his name, his vision.**

She took her place as **the honorary president of the Musée Christian-Dior**, ensuring that the world would never forget **the boy who had once sketched dresses in the margins of notebooks, who had turned fabric into poetry.**

She lived to see his name **become immortal.**

And when she passed in 2008, she did so knowing that her brother's name would live **forever.**

Even in death, Christian Dior remained a **man of mystery.**

A man who had lived by **omens, who had trusted in tarot cards and lucky charms, who had consulted the unseen before every great decision.**

Had he **always known?**

Had he felt it coming, in the whispers of the wind, in the flickering of candlelight, in the way fate had always left him little clues?

Or was it all just **coincidence**—the inevitable passing of time, the fragile nature of life itself?

No one would ever know for sure.

But one thing remained certain:

Christian Dior had not just **lived.**

He had built.

He had built an empire, a dream, a vision of femininity that transcended time.

He had built **not just dresses, but a world.**

And though he was gone, **his legacy remained.**

In every stitch.

In every bottle of Miss Dior.

In every woman who stepped into a Dior gown and felt, for a moment, like she had stepped into **something magical.**

Christian Dior had once said,

"Deep in every heart slumbers a dream, and the couturier knows it: every woman is a princess."

And in the world he left behind, **every woman still was.**

Because Dior, the man, was gone.

But Dior, the dream, would never die.

Epilogue: The Eternal Fragrance

A scent is never just a scent.

It is **a memory**, bottled and preserved, lingering long after its wearer has gone.

Long after Christian Dior took his final bow, **Miss Dior still lingers.**

A whisper of jasmine in the air. A trace of rose on the skin. A presence felt but unseen.

It is more than perfume.

It is **a love letter, a tribute, a bond that transcends time.**

The fragrance was born from **Catherine's resilience**, from Christian's longing to capture something that could never be taken away—**their past, their childhood, their survival.**

And now, it drifts through the world, unseen but unmistakable, as if Catherine is still walking through the flower markets of Paris, as if Christian is still standing in his atelier, adjusting the fold of a silk gown with a perfectionist's touch.

Miss Dior was created for **one woman**, yet it belongs to **all women.**

Every drop carries the echo of Catherine's strength, the vision of Christian's artistry.

Every woman who wears it, knowingly or not, carries a part of their story.

A part of their **Parisian fairytale.**

Time moves forward, but **some things refuse to be forgotten.**

Christian and Catherine's journey—from the rose-filled gardens of Granville to the glittering salons of Paris, from the shadows of war to the golden age of couture—**is stitched into history.**

It is in the sketches preserved in museum archives.

In the gowns that still command awe on runways.

In the letters Christian wrote, filled with the quiet poetry of a man who lived for beauty.

And in the way his name remains, not just in fashion, but in **culture, in artistry, in the very idea of what it means to dream.**

They were two souls shaped by the same past, two halves of the same memory, bound together by something deeper than fate.

Christian built **Dior**, but he built it on **love—love for elegance, love for art, love for a sister who had survived what should have broken her.**

And that kind of love does not fade.

Granville: Where It All Began

Today, visitors to **Villa Les Rhumbs, the childhood home of Christian and Catherine,** can still walk through the gardens.

The same gardens where **a young boy once stood in wonder, surrounded by the roses that would shape his destiny.**

The same paths where Catherine ran barefoot, her laughter trailing behind her like perfume on the wind.

The roses still bloom there, untouched by time.

And if you stand still long enough, if you close your eyes and let the sea breeze carry you back, **you might just smell the lingering trace of something familiar.**

Not just flowers.

Not just perfume.

But **a story.**

A story of resilience and beauty, of loss and triumph, of fashion and love.

A story that, like **Miss Dior**, will never truly disappear.

Appendices:

Timeline of Significant Events in Christian and Catherine Dior's Lives

Early Years (1905–1930s)
- **1905, January 21** – Christian Dior is born in Granville, Normandy, France.
- **1917** – The Dior family moves to Paris.
- **1920s** – Christian Dior develops a passion for art and dreams of becoming an architect.
- **1928** – Christian opens an art gallery in Paris, showcasing works by Picasso, Dalí, and Giacometti. The Great Depression forces its closure.
- **1935** – To make ends meet, Dior begins selling fashion sketches to Parisian designers.
- **1937** – He joins Robert Piguet's fashion house as a designer.

World War II and the Shadows of War (1940–1945)
- **1940** – Dior is conscripted into military service at the start of World War II.
- **1941** – Catherine Dior joins the French Resistance, secretly working against the Nazi occupation.
- **1942** – Christian returns to Paris and works for couturier Lucien Lelong, designing dresses for Nazi officers' wives while secretly helping the Resistance.

- **1944, July 6** – Catherine is **arrested by the Gestapo**, tortured, and deported to the Ravensbrück concentration camp.
- **1945, May 28** – Catherine is **liberated and returns to France**, physically devastated but unbroken in spirit.

The Birth of the House of Dior (1946–1950s)

- **1946** – With backing from textile magnate Marcel Boussac, Christian Dior establishes his own fashion house at **30 Avenue Montaigne**.
- **1947, February 12** – Dior presents his first collection, introducing the **"New Look"**, which revolutionizes post-war fashion.
- **1947** – Christian launches **"Miss Dior"** perfume, named in honor of Catherine.
- **1950s** – The House of Dior expands worldwide, becoming synonymous with Parisian elegance.

Christian Dior's Final Years and Legacy (1954–1957)

- **1954** – Dior publishes his autobiography, *Dior by Dior*.
- **1955** – He mentors young designer **Yves Saint Laurent**, who would later take over the fashion house.
- **1957, October 24** – Christian Dior dies unexpectedly of a heart attack in Montecatini, Italy. He is 52 years old.

Catherine Dior's Later Life and Dedication to Her Brother's Legacy (1957–2008)

- **1960s–1980s** – Catherine runs a **flower business in Paris**, supplying blooms to the House of Dior.
- **1988** – She becomes the **honorary president of the Musée Christian Dior**, dedicated to preserving her brother's legacy.
- **2008, June 17** – Catherine Dior passes away at the age of 90.

Fashion Terms

Fashion Terms

- **Atelier** – A designer's workshop or studio where garments are created, often by skilled seamstresses and tailors.
- **A-Line** – A silhouette that flares out gradually from the waist, creating the shape of the letter "A"; a staple of Dior's later designs
- **Bar Suit** – Christian Dior's most iconic design from his 1947 collection, featuring a cinched waist, padded hips, and a voluminous skirt. It became the defining look of the "New Look" era.
- **Bias Cut** – A method of cutting fabric diagonally across the grain to create fluidity and drape, popularized by designers like Madeleine Vionnet.
- **Couture** – Derived from the French word for "sewing," couture refers to the art of designing and making high-end, custom-fitted clothing.
- **Couturier** – A designer who creates custom-made fashion pieces, particularly in the world of haute couture.

- **Draping** – The art of positioning and pinning fabric on a mannequin or model to create the desired shape before it is sewn.
- **Demi-Couture** – A hybrid between haute couture and ready-to-wear; garments are still handcrafted but are more accessible than custom couture pieces.
- **Empire Waist** – A high-waisted silhouette where the bodice ends just below the bust, with the rest of the dress flowing loosely downward.
- **Ensemble** – A complete outfit, typically including matching garments and accessories.
- **Fashion Illustration** – A hand-drawn representation of a garment or collection, often used for design conceptualization before garments are produced.
- **Flou** – A French term used in couture to refer to the art of soft dressmaking, contrasting with the structured tailoring of men's suiting.
- **Garment Construction** – The techniques and processes used to assemble a piece of clothing, from pattern-making to final stitching.
- **Grosgrain Ribbon** – A fabric with tightly ribbed texture often used in couture for trims, waistbands, and structural reinforcement.
- **Haute Couture** – Meaning "high sewing" in French, haute couture refers to the exclusive fashion industry where garments are handcrafted from luxurious materials and tailored to fit individual clients.
- **Hemline** – The edge of a garment, often used to describe the length of a dress or skirt.
- **Lookbook** – A collection of styled photographs showcasing a designer's latest collection.
- **Ligne Corolle** – The original name for Dior's **New Look**, meaning "corolla line," referring to the shape of flower petals.
- **Maison de Couture** – A fashion house that produces high-end, custom garments, like the House of Dior.

- **Mannequin** – In couture, this term is often used for models who present garments at fashion shows and private fittings.
- **New Look** – Dior's groundbreaking 1947 collection that introduced a return to femininity after World War II, characterized by cinched waists and full skirts.
- **Pattern-Making** – The process of creating templates for fabric pieces before a garment is assembled.
- **Peplum** – A short, flared fabric panel that extends from the waist, adding volume and shape to a garment.
- **Plissé** – A fabric treatment that creates permanent pleats, often used in evening gowns.
- **Ready-to-Wear (Prêt-à-Porter)** – Unlike haute couture, ready-to-wear refers to factory-made clothing produced in standard sizes for the mass market.
- **Silhouette** – The overall shape of a garment on the body, defining its structure and volume.
- **Surrealism** – An artistic movement that influenced Dior's early career, characterized by dreamlike, avant-garde aesthetics.
- **Tailoring** – The craft of constructing structured, precisely fitted garments, often associated with men's suiting but essential in haute couture.
- **Toile** – A prototype garment made from inexpensive fabric, used to test a design before creating the final version.
- **Trompe-l'œil** – A visual illusion in art and fashion where garments are designed to trick the eye into seeing texture or depth that isn't actually present.

Notable Figures in Dior's Journey

Christian Dior (1905–1957)
   The central figure of this narrative, Dior revolutionized post-war fashion with his 1947 **New Look**, bringing back opulence, femininity, and elegance to women's wardrobes. His visionary approach to fashion transformed the House of Dior into an enduring empire.

Catherine Dior (1917–2008)
   Christian's beloved sister, Catherine was a **French Resistance fighter** who survived **Ravensbrück concentration camp**. Her resilience inspired the fragrance **Miss Dior**, named in her honor.

Marcel Boussac (1889–1980)
   A powerful French textile magnate who financed the creation of the **House of Dior** in 1946. Without his investment, Christian Dior's dream may never have come to fruition.

Pierre Cardin (1922–2020)
   Worked as Dior's **head tailor** before founding his own fashion empire. Cardin was instrumental in crafting the **New Look** garments with Dior's signature structured silhouettes.

Jean Cocteau (1889–1963)
   Poet, playwright, and artist, Cocteau was one of Dior's closest friends and artistic inspirations, introducing him to **the avant-garde art scene** in Paris.

Robert Piguet (1898–1953)
   Swiss-born designer who gave Dior one of his first jobs in fashion. Under Piguet, Dior refined his style, learning the importance of **simplicity and elegance** in design.

Lucien Lelong (1889–1958)
   French couturier and influential mentor to Dior. He kept French

fashion alive during World War II and protected young designers like Dior from being sent to Germany.

Yves Saint Laurent (1936–2008)

Dior's **protégé and successor,** taking over the House of Dior after Christian's sudden death. Saint Laurent carried Dior's legacy into the next era of fashion.

Mitzah Bricard (1900–1977)

Dior's **muse and confidante,** known for her extravagant style, love of leopard print, and unwavering devotion to elegance. She helped define the **mystique of Dior's brand.**

Salvador Dalí (1904–1989)

A surrealist artist who influenced Dior's artistic vision. Dior collaborated with Dalí on projects that fused **fashion and Surrealism.**

Coco Chanel (1883–1971)

One of Dior's greatest rivals, Chanel dismissed the New Look, claiming it set women back by decades. Their **contrasting visions of femininity** shaped the future of fashion.

www.ingramcontent.com/pod-product-compliance
Lightning Source LLC
LaVergne TN
LVHW020433080526
838202LV00055B/5168

9 7 8 4 4 4 6 9 7 9 0 9 0